This Ecstasy They Call
DAMNATION

poems by Israel Wasserstein

ALSO FROM WOODLEY PRESS

Begin Again: 150 Kansas Poems
Edited by Caryn Mirriam-Goldberg

Mythology of Touch
by Mary Stone Dockery

Fire Mobile: Pregnancy Sonnets
by Matthew Porubsky

Kansas Poems of William Stafford
Edited by Denise Low

This Ecstasy They Call
DAMNATION

poems by Israel Wasserstein

WOODLEY PRESS

Editor Dennis Etzel Jr.
Copyright ©2012 Israel Wasserstein
Printed by Lightning Source
Cover Art: "Night Air" by Jennifer Rivera
Used with the artist's permission

      Book Design by Leah Sewell
      lsewell.tumblr.com/

Woodley Press
Department of English
Washburn University
Topeka, KS 66621
http://www.washburn.edu/reference/woodley-press/

ISBN: 978-0-9828752-8-5

for Liz

ACKNOWLEDGEMENTS

My thanks to the following publications, where the following poems first appeared (sometimes in different versions or with different titles):

"Highway 54: Happy Land" and "Love Song of Fergus"
     - *BorderSenses*
"Watching Citizen Kane" - *Conceptions Southwest*
"One Way to Play the Blues" - *Flint Hills Review*
"Foxwife Hunted" and "Trailer Park Winter" - *Inscape*
"How it is for Eyeless Things in Caves" - *Iota*
"Adam," "Eve," "Lilith," "Cain," "Abel," and "Angel at the Gate of Eden"
     - *Red Mesa Review*
"Domesticity," "Eclipse," "Foxwife" and "Serenity" - *seveneightfive*
"Job Fishes with his Friend" and "Witness"
     - *RowHouse Poetry Revue*
"Jess Willard Apologizes to Jack Johnson" - *Coal City Review*
"John Brown" - *KansasPoets.com*
"Coffee with Zeus," "The Gods Play Poker," and "Stepping into the Woods"
     - *Fickle Muses*
"Meditations on the Preserved" - *Blue Mesa Review*
"Theodicy" - *FutureCycle Poetry*
"A Kansas Native Discusses Natural Disasters" and "Highway 54: Controlled Burn"
     - *Begin Again: 150 Kansas Poems*

INTRODUCTION

I am happy to introduce Israel Wasserstein's poems as a colleague, friend, and admirer. It hasn't been an easy task to sum up the complexity of this work, the layered textures that ask for reading after reading, to uncover what is there. Just as the prairie relies on the small and the unseen for her life, these poems breathe on different sea levels.

This collection is a journey with several paths, via the mythological, the personal, the political, and the literal road: Highway 54. Israel finished his MFA down in New Mexico, so these poem-markers of Highway 54—the highway that runs through Kansas down to New Mexico—serve as "mile stones" of growth, figurative and literal, for the voice in this collection—for the reader's imagination and passengership.

There is a lot of prairie that leads into desert along 54, and these poems have their share of earth-sky divisions and intersections in creating a Great Plains mythos. There is a lot of sun in these poems, like in the opening poem "One Way to Play the Blues": "*It doesn't hurt./* He'd repeat the old lie, his hand steady, / his eyes squinting against the sun." Both the physiological and psychological effects of the sun are a part of the Midwestern psyche, and these poems are reflections of that deeper part of being human:

> You pray, slow, measured,
>
> bend down to scoop dust
>
> into your sun-lined hand,
>
> then rise to pour
>
> it like water from between
>
> your fingers. ("Praying for Rain")

Just as the metaphorical juxtaposition of weather is included, so is the awareness of rain in these works, often on any Kansan's mind:

> Eastern Kansas, hills pungent
>
> with controlled burn...
>
> ...Sunglasses

conceal their eyes
as they watch the sky,

the night clear,
free of portentous clouds.
Rain will not come. ("Highway 54: Controlled Burn")

This psyche of the Great Plains, informed by weather, speaks of hardships and relief.

However, there is also earth, what the prairie has to offer. This creates the juxtaposition of earth and sky—translating into love. Personally, I know Israel wrote this poem to whom this collection is dedicated to, and he metaphorically succeeds:

But now I know: you are a child of land.
Amidst its tremors you brace under doorframes

without fear. I was raised by sky,
its furies as much as its calms.
("A Kansas Native Discusses Natural Disasters")

This final line summarizes the wisdom in these poems—the balance of fury and calmness.

Throughout these trials and connections of sky and earth, the mythos that touches with its fingertips, the historically mythological comes to touch us, too. Place what you know aside, as these figures come from the distant horizon to speak to us: "Let's say you're god, and things have gotten off / to a rough start, with the Angels and all" ("Theodicy"). Via dramatic monologues, we hear from each immortalized person, each story that reflects each of our struggles in the world:

But one thing: escaping His curse,
I claimed the grit of life, all the mysteries
His foolish children call *myth*. Mine

are tales told in darkness, cries
of my children, those who drink deeply
from the cup of pleasure and pain

and savor the gift ordained for them:

this ecstasy they call damnation. ("Lilith")

These mythologies are brought into the mythos in the fashion scholars Eva M. Thury and Margaret K. Devinney describe: mythological stories as narratives that reflect a perception of the world. Through the dramatic monologue, the reader shares the "I" voice—the self that travels to connect with the mystical.

I overheard Israel speaking to Denise Low-Weso after a talk she gave over what makes a Kansas poet. There was something said by Israel about someone's comment on the subtlety in his work. Yes, there is the subtle, but the mystical, poetic strength in this collection stretches past definition. Maybe this is a work of a contemporary mythology as well, as we follow the journey away from home and back again, just as Joseph Campbell discovered in his Hero's Journey.

There is something aloof in this work, something that comes from a deeper voice speaking, and I celebrate and am deeply thankful for Israel's openness and fierce wrestling in each of these poems. Just like the angel that visited Jacob, Israel is holding on, getting to what can't simply be said.

Dennis Etzel Jr.
Woodley Press
April 2012

CONTENTS

IV   **71**

'Read poems as prayers,' he said
                    —Seamus Heaney, "Station Island"

I.

ONE WAY TO PLAY THE BLUES
for Matthew

These long summer afternoons
he thumbs guitar strings
until his fingers blister—slow,
sad love songs, lots of minor keys.
                              His teacher
tells him, *touch 'em beat-quick*
to a hot burner, you'll
callous 'em right up.
                              He remembers
those same afternoons, years past,
the grass behind his trailer grown high
as his waist, but beaten
down by sun and treadless sneakers.
He'd press his back to the rotting
wood of the tool shed, breathe
the smell of mildew, watch kicked-up
dust stir in the doorframe,
and finger a stolen lighter, metal
cool in his hands.
                              Then he'd click
it to life, its flame sputtering blue
and yellow, run it under his palm,
practicing for his friends.
                              It doesn't hurt.
He'd repeat the old lie, his hand steady,
his eyes squinting against the sun.

Trailer Park Winter

Mornings, hungry for heat,
I'd curl beside the vent,
press my eight-year-old body
to warm metal. Mother stepped
heavily through the trailer,
joints creaking. Wind
whistled through windows,
each breath clouded before me.

A stray cat made her home
beneath that vent,
birthed a litter of kittens.
At night we'd hear them
mewing, their cries slicing
through the walls. My father forbade
us to feed them. *Feed them once,*
he said, *and they'll stay
'til they starve.*

The mother's black coat
was knotted with blood. She walked
with a limp, her right forepaw
dragging, useless. The trailer park
was overrun, cats everywhere. Older
boys hurled rocks at them
and the man who lived three houses up
sat in a lawn chair
with a pellet gun, waiting.

Behind us, a woman with a No Trespassing
sign peered through windows,
breath misting on the glass. Her dog growled,
choked himself straining against his chain
when someone walked by. I hiked
long circuits to avoid him.

The cats, too, avoided that trailer.
Winter had its small blessings
for them. When the worst
cold forced us inside, they
slinked through the park,
unmolested. Snow offered shelter,
piled so thick I thought I'd lose
myself in the drifts.
Hands which touched
metal had to be yanked away,
leaving behind frozen bits of skin.

One by one, the kittens froze.
The mother cat left long before winter did.
Still I pressed a red ear
to the vent, listening.

I heard only the groan of floorboards
as mother worked in the kitchen. Steam swirled
from oatmeal on the stove.
Her hands shook
when she wasn't rubbing them together,
the burn of friction not enough, not even then.

A KANSAS NATIVE DISCUSSES
NATURAL DISASTERS

Raised in California, you freeze with each storm warning,
listen for the locomotive roar,
imagine the funnel cloud descending
dark against greenblack dusk.

Strange, I thought. You know
the earth can swallow cars, houses,
that land can collapse to sea,
that the next Big One is inevitable.

Yet a twister might pass blocks away
and leave us unaware 'til sirens woke us.
But now I know: you are a child of land.
Amidst its tremors you brace under doorframes

without fear. I was raised by sky,
its furies as much as its calms.
When the evening chills with the hammer of hail,
the air takes me breathless, tense, home.

Birthing Pains

The air is gravid with storm:
I feel it coming,
shiver in August heat.
Before Kansas storms, all
is silent. I remember

myself, eight, eager to meet
a promised sibling.
When the call from the hospital
came, I shouted *I've got
a new baby brother.*
But the babysitter's
eyes gave me pause.

At last the storm breaks
free, screaming its rage
in thunder, hissing wind.
Rain soaks my skin.

The hospital hall echoed
with buzzing lights. I had to see
for myself, could find no tears
for what I could not understand.
He lingered for a while.
The storm raged outside,
clattering on distant windows.

SERENITY

is the night we saw
lamplight flooding through
oak leaves thick and dark
as avocadoes

or the way everything stills
before the summer storm
clamors around that oak

or the next morning
when water pools lazily
and maybe you smile
and go back to sleep

but never never is it eternal
or perfect
at best, it is enough

just unexpected moments,
the burn of your lips
against my cheek,

the way you touched me
like it meant something.

HIGHWAY 54: HAPPY LAND

Welcome to Happy Land Trailer Park,
reads a rust-heavy sign wreathed
in shattered neon bulbs.

Strung across this stretch of highway
between unplanted fields and feedyards,
it wears the silence of dead cars,

of bikes with shattered frames.
Vacant-eyed trailers stare across the road,
a few with signs of life—a plant wilting

in a window, moth-eaten curtains,
a basketball goal listing sharply. Someone
maintains a weary garden, fighting

for life against rocky topsoil.
Years past, someone dreamed this place
prosperous, dreamed a coming boom,

and owners believed, believed and followed.
Car frames on cinder blocks and screen
doors hanging half open: these are their legacy.

Most have drifted off to some
more optimistic place, one free
of the smell of cows and mattress mold,

yet a few remain like the vines that creep
up their trailers, withered, wind-twisted,
still hanging on.

Domesticity

Repetition's gentle prodding
teaches him the value of small miracles:
wet scent of grass, rainbowed
steam rising from dishes.

In the silence of that house
he finds order in the mundane:
wake, furrow through the garden,
prune each tree
with a surgeon's hand.
Then, indoors, scrub, vacuum, make lunch.

For two winter weeks,
sun slices across bare floor, halos
the faded picture resting
on a dresser in the unused room.

He has learned
to change his routine
on those cold days, and never enters
that room except to dust,
keep things straight.
From photos she smiles,
her hair still rich enough to live on.

During long afternoons, his work done,
he wanders through the caverns
of the house. Dust motes drift
in waning light.

ECLIPSE

Earth's shadow swallows a Hunter's
Moon, and light-drowned stars reappear
one by one above the desert.

A cloud drifts across sky,
obscures Orion. As darkness drinks
the sun's reflection, the moon

diminishes. Its dark mass, wreathed
in orange, is extinguished, as if retreating
from our weight. Years now since

the last eclipse, since the night
you tired of this planet's flicker.
There is comfort in the way the moon

darkens and returns, the old rites
still intact. A feeling, too,
of permanence, masterful illusion.

Yet somewhere, a billion light-years away,
a star exhausts its fuel, collapses.
All things end in absolute zero.

Alone under an empty sky, I'll mourn
our loss in my own small way: a few words
written under a veiled moon,

as coyotes call across
the desert, on a night
much like any other, on a planet

chasing itself through the darkness
we each know so well.

VISITED

[Sodom] was destroyed . . . for the sin of inhospitality to strangers.
—John Boswell

They came to us one evening,
two big dogs, one black
against the night, the other dull
gray as the road.

Though their coats and paws
were marred with cuts, with blood,
these beautiful ones
waited, passive, silent.

They paced outside the door,
dark eyes asking
for entrance. But we could not:
our cat was enraged,

our beagle, terrified, the children,
wordless and intimidated.
Yet we ached to see them, stoic
and alone, asking for help,

but not begging. And, remembering
we might entertain angels unaware,
we did what we could, gave them food,
water, blankets to keep out the cold.

We waited for morning to find
them new homes, to grant some relief
for those weary travelers.
At dawn (I had felt it),

they were gone. We told ourselves
we had done all we could,
though we'd left visitors
on the doorstep when we turned inside,

toward Sodom, toward Gomorrah.

THE NEXT MORNING

We did not wake in the cold grip of morning,
never suffered side by side
the loneliness of hangover
as black coffee burned our throats.

That night when longing did not unravel
to realization or disappointment,
did you see what I took so long
to discover, that Tantalus' fate

was not all punishment? Though
his tongue burned inside his mouth,
though his lips shriveled and cracked,
to drink was worse, to drink and find

satisfaction a myth. That night
you began to teach me:
to desire is to be unfulfilled, and fullness
as heat of bodies in the night,

empties again and always into hunger.

WITNESS
for my Father

Heat roared from pavement, and you almost passed
unaware. Yet the scene caught you:
a woman seemed to sleep in a car's simmering
cabin, motionless save for the rise
and fall of her belly, heavy with pregnancy.
Then a tear slid down her inflamed cheek.

When the ambulance arrived, the paramedics
said it was a diabetic reaction. The next day
she would tell you how, frozen and aware,
she heard you approach, felt your shadow fall
across her. *It was a miracle,*
she said, *that you came by.*

But first you returned
to your apartment, where your wife
and sons slept through the burning afternoon,
unborn child perhaps asleep as well.
A fan buzzed in the window. The drape-shrouded
room closed around you. Shafts of light caught
dust motes, released them to darkness.
When we rose, one by one, blinking,
and shuffled from the bedroom,
we found you motionless, waiting, twilight
angled around your darkened frame.

II.

STEPPING INTO THE WOODS

Turn around. The woods have swallowed
you already. The way in is easier
than the way out. Obey these rules:

stay on the path. Do not follow the lights
that flicker on the edge of sight.
Do not eat the bread crumbs,

or listen to the voices, though they echo
through you like the promise of home.
Begin to forget that word: it's only

a place you return to and find
no longer exists. Like a cabin
braced with candy canes, lovely

to see, dangerous to touch.
You'll meet strangers on the way.
Speak to them if you must,

but give them nothing, tell them nothing.
What sharp teeth they have.
Others have come here

before you, but few have left. Curiosity
can consume you. You may think
you see your parents, your lover.

Do not run to them. If you come to a cabin
with legs, walk past it. The skittering
behind you may grow distant in time.

Try not to dream of what may have been.
Distrust what you see. Remember the tale
of the girl who took the stranger's

generosity, how he dragged her
through the streets in a spiked barrel,
or chewed her bones clean. Learn

that trust can kill, that death
is not the worst thing that can happen
to the young. If you must sleep,

do not dream. The woods enfold
you now, thick as blankets. I tell
you the truth: they are patient

as wolves, hungry as winter.

FOXWIFE

When you slipped your skin
for one you loved
incompletely, as a voice, a gesture,

when you left your den,
your family, a thousand scents
and the forest's twisting trails,

when you took up a life
you knew nothing of, stepped naked
into all you thought you wanted,

did you find what you sought
amidst his strange language,
the night air made unfamiliar?

Tell me, Foxwife,
of stepping into a new life,
how a body falls away,

tell me all you found in its place.

Picnic Scene with Gods

It's Thursday, and the gods
gather in the park. Zeus flies
a kite, hoping for sparks.

Anubis watches, his face
long. *Wait and see,*
he says, shaking his cane,

kids today! and sits down.
Demeter hoards the fruit
basket, casts angry glances

at suspicious young men.
Take Loki, for instance,
with broad smile

and cunning face. He taunts
his brother, who never even
notices. He's too busy ogling

the women, a few
of the men. Lilith lets
her eyes travel Demeter's

body. If only she weren't
so uptight, if only she didn't
hold herself like a prick.

Morrigan and Backlum-Chaam
are drunk and fighting. Hoof-prints
lead away from them. *Don't*

demean me, he shouts.
She picks at a limp hotdog, grins.
Athena can't resist

an *I told you so*. Beside her,
a bush burns, a man in white
rolls his eyes, adjusts his halo.

Coyote slips away from Abassi,
shaking creation's keys.
Abassi's grin is ripe with knowledge.

He winks to Persephone,
saunters off to find his wife,
to pinch her ass, whisper in her ear.

THE GODS PLAY POKER

Three in the morning, the room reeks
of incense and cow blood, and they're
just looking for a break. They've told

their women they can't go out tonight.
Sunday's card night,
the only time they get to see the guys.

Even Osiris made it, though it's damn hard to stack
chips through all those bandages, and Isis
is at home, pissed. He's into his sixth

glass of something strong, something he can't identify,
but he's finally feeling good. Shit,
he says, *a woman sews your dick back on, it ain't easy*

to tell her no. Bacchus stamps his foot in approval,
shuffles his chips. He's down five bucks, will win it back
when the other gods are *in their cups,*

as Balor puts it. He's been holding up the game,
afraid to look at his cards, but no one says anything:
even Gods know better than to pick fights

with one-eyed giants. Jesus keeps hitting
bad cards. He sips wine, mutters *Eli, Eli*
under his breath. Peter's been pestering him

for an invite. Since he's infallible, has keys
to heaven, he thinks he qualifies, but they refuse:
what's a club where anyone can join?

There's been a stir recently, some trickster
with a Vaseline smile calling himself a god,
holding forth at the Casino Buffet, dealing

Aces to anyone who asks. The gods agree,
say his type is small time, but Zeus isn't so sure.
He's got a splitting headache, is all in

with a low pair. He's getting older,
learning what worship's all about,
how much someone would give to turn

things around, just for a minute, just
to show that beautiful Ace of Spades,
scoop that pile of chips, call yourself

blessed, for one hand, blessed.

Highway 54: El Dorado Lake

When the Army flooded the gorge
to create the lake,
they didn't bother to cut down
the trees that grew there.

You can still see them along
the highway, bone-white trunks,
lifeless branches twisted
toward sky, stretching
across the gray surface.

If you follow this road west,
you will come to Texas
and a withered gulch, old
stream-bed with a swath
of barren trees, water
barely remembered.

Otherwise the landscape is flat,
featureless. Nothing grows
more than a few feet off the ground.

I have driven this path dozens
of times, will trace it many
more. I know the shape of each
rotten stump, try to imagine histories
for them, histories for this place,
but my imagination fails: I can see
only that they are dead,
dead but still standing.

Coffee with Zeus

Anything can be a god if you're not careful,
he says. Behind him, clouds crawl
over the mountain, drop into the valley
like petitioners.
                              It starts big enough.
They make deities for the usual things:
weather, war, women, that lot.
Soon enough they might be worshiping
spoons, boys with stringed instruments
and funny hair. Before you know it,
they hardly remember you
until you remind them.
                              Thunder rolls
its promise over us. In the cramped
café, no one even looks up.
                              You see?
Even the pyrotechnics don't awe them
anymore. I'd rather be a god of sports.
Plenty of postulants there. Or, hell,
a god of famine and abundance. There's
never a shortage of starvation.

He picks at his muffin, complete
with its own stormcloud.
                              You get comfortable,
that's the problem, and they're gone
before you even know to miss them.
They can't even worship properly any more—
their new gods are sterile, shrink-wrapped
things. Not that we were much better.

He stands, his robes billow about
him, wind-tossed.
                    I need to go.
The wife wants me back by nine.
As if women even want me now.

He slips down an alley, rain leaping
off his shoulders. A child plays
in the torrent. Zeus rubs the boy's
hair, blue sparks jumping from his fingers.

LOVE SONG OF FERGUS

Who will go drive with Fergus now,
And pierce the deep wood's woven shade,
And dance upon the level shore?
        —Yeats

Pass me and know me not:
I, who once was king, now sleep
in clearings wrapped in restless stars.

For years I kept my kingdom
with sword-arm, but man
grows weary of battle,

and each night my tower
closed around me.
If I grew old and discontent,

and each morning I woke
from restless sleep,
if the forest whispered

my name, if evening
grew heavy with the ache
of open spaces, and the oldest

song called me west,
west toward the sea,
who was I to resist?

Listen: the night is wide,
and everywhere the echo
of countryside and thicket

calls to us, brothers, sisters,
urges us to seek ourselves
in shrouded corners of the world.

Foxwife Hunted

Her lover's wife sends men to trample
trails in search of her. They bring

dogs who roar their eagerness through
the forest, guns breathing fire

from angry mouths, pursue her endlessly.
Finally, cornered, caught between baying

and memory of her lover's eyes,
she is not the fox

who left the forest, nor the woman
rejected for a wife returned.

The hunter-smells grow closer. She begins
to change, paws lengthening, smoothing,

snout receding. Her orange-red hair
shortens like wheat gathered up

by wicked scythes. Alone
now, without the scent of forest,

without her swift paws, without even
the naïve certainty of her human youth,

she waits for the end. The forest closes
around her, branches reaching

for her like the hungry arms of men.

SPELUNKER

He left nothing behind, not a scrap
of clothing or his name scrawled
in limestone. The caves offered no clue

he had entered. He told his friends
he'd be back, ignited his flashlight,
and stepped into darkness.

They never interviewed his classmates,
sullen-eyed boys failing math
and girls with wrinkled dresses.

The slick-haired reporters
preferred relatives and friends
in coordinated black and gray,

or businessmen with over-creased
suits, ties a bit awry,
who speak in perfect soundbites.

The national guard pulled up behind
the media trucks, lit the caves
like sunrise, sent eyeless things scattering,

confused by lights hot as the land
their ancestors abandoned
many forgotten generations past.

His best friend, all sandy
hair and freckles,
will write his own story

one bright December,
the sun scorching his frosted
skin, a story where his friend slips

quietly beneath the earth,
burrowing away from winter,
to tunnels too small

for grown men, lit
by oddly luminescent
things, unfamiliar things.

He makes his friend a daring
spelunker (he rolls the word
over his tongue) still far

too busy to come up
and share with the world
all he's seen. His mother

finds his tale, fears for his safety,
and watches the paper curl
and burn. Ashes rise over

the barren trees, the silent caves,
and two girls, who whisper
their own story

as snow begins to fall.

LAZARUS

Three days I lay dead in the tomb.
Three days, and now they
look to me with wary eyes,

as if they want to ask, but are afraid.
I understand their fear, though
You brought me back, pulled me
squinting into the world of the living,

into the morning heat.
You could tell me, if you chose,
what I learned in the tomb

and lost in donning my skin.
I remember so little—darkness,
a wind which howled, howled,
and muffled by the wind, words.

As I try to recapture them, they slip
from me, always at the edge
of thought, just beyond reach.

You, too, have come from death
and returned, scars etched
across your body. You must have heard
the words. Will you at last speak?

Tell me what there is to learn in darkness
and the storm, in all I wished to know,
all I could not hold.

WHAT THE DEAD WANT

You. It has always been
you. By now, you must know that.
When did understanding dawn?

When you heard the groans
of a hundred caskets shattered at once?
When our hands emerged, bloody,

splintered, maggot-dripping? As you watched
us shamble up the hill, each step
a struggle: bones snapping, flesh

peeling like rotten fruit?
Tell us you've always
known. See what we endure

for you. Everything is an obstacle now:
doorknobs once turned so easily,
now baffle our clumsy hands. Each movement

is agony, yet we'll batter ourselves
against doors, walls, whatever keeps us from you.
We have nothing but time—

if god won't call us, we'll make do.
Exhaust yourself running from us.
It will do no good, it never has. We remember

your smell. You slept with our spouses,
you were our spouses.
While you live, we can never forget,

can never be satisfied. We are ravenous
for the ripeness of your bodies,
the feel of flesh in our mouths.

III.

THEODICY
after Kim Addonizio

Let's say you're god, and things have gotten off
to a rough start, with the Angels and all.
Just when you think you've got it right, a couple
of naked humans, a garden, everything
goes to hell. It wasn't supposed to be hard:
eat, fuck, name the damn animals. So the tree
may have been a mistake, but even you
didn't know how bad everything would go.
But there's this guy Job, and he's alright, sends
you nice notes, doesn't kick small animals
or screw around on his wife. Then Satan
shows up, starts talking shit, says, sure Job's fine,
he's got a pretty sweet deal. You start thinking
if he's right then this creation stuff wasn't
worth a damn anyway. You take the bet,
and next thing you know Job's in sack cloth. His friends
won't leave him alone, tell him this is your fault,
or his, that he's evil or unlucky.
Job doesn't know what to think, you don't know
what to think. Now you're wondering if you
made a big mistake, if Job's worship
was fine before he lost everything. You're
about to break down, sort this mess out,
or maybe start over, and then someone
tells a story about Job. So it's not
the way it happened, so it says
you planned it all, so it says Satan's
an asshole and you're a hero,
though you created him, so Job comes off
a little too good: people are listening,
talking, praying, writing. They're just as fucked up
as ever, but there's something new and beautiful
in this, something you can't place. The worse

things get the more they have to say, and you
know it's a lie and you're not sure
you should encourage this, but there it is,
there they are, eating, fucking, talking about you,
about Job, and you're not about to look away.

THIS POEM IS NOT ABOUT YOU

though you think it is. When I write
that you are stooped now, reading
these lines, that outside the rain
has ceased, and water lies
in oil-wrapped puddles,

it is mere coincidence. To be right
is no great achievement. I tell you
that yesterday you kissed the one
you could love, or wished to kiss:
this takes no great genius.

When your lover caresses the small
of your back, you shiver, your breath catches.
This poem is like your lover's touch.
Though it has never met you, it knows

to whisper in your ear, to draw itself
slowly across your skin. This poem
wants to introduce itself to you,
to make you fall in
and out of love

with it a hundred times. This poem
wants to shout at you from across
the house, to hear the words
you whisper in your sleep. This poem
wants to know you the way

I know you: imperfectly, yet well enough
to make you close your eyes and shudder.

Praying for Rain

The farmers gather, their worn
faces in a semi-circle,
wives and children in their Sunday
best behind, somber eyes
hinting at hope. You step into the center,
leather boots beaten craggy
as your face, as the twisted
cracks of your Bible's cover.

Each step stirs dirt
from the hungry field, whispering
through withered stalks
of corn. The wind
has worn the silo to the flat
color of rust.
Trees lean, leafless. Branches
scrape a desperate hymn
as you speak, your voice grating
over long-memorized passages.

You pray, slow, measured,
bend down to scoop dust
into your sun-lined hand,
then rise to pour
it like water from between
your fingers. Wind catches
and blows it over
fields, homes, exultant
families, their eyes raised,
who watch the empty sky
in rapturous silence.

ADAM

The ground wet with morning, I breathe
field-must, greening
scent of furrows. Behind me

the angel's sword burns
like dawn, casts my long
shadow across earth.

When the gates closed
behind us, my wife turned
from me, the serpent

slithered away. I thought
I would hate the earth,
the labor assigned to me.

Now I lay these seeds
in rows. They will sprout, grow:
some will thrive, others

wilt, and I will plant
again. I remember the garden,
each fruit sprung

fully-formed, unborn,
unbearing. Sweat beads
on my brow. Before death,

there was no birth. I bend down,
scoop earth in my hands.
It welcomes me, cools

my sun-beaten skin.

EVE

Some say before me was another
whose crime, perhaps, was fucking
with more passion than my dear
husband (who rushed

to blame this faulty rib). She
disappeared beyond the garden's
walls, to somewhere cold
and barren, a punishment.

One day, the damp air
clung to my skin.
Trees crowded down.
Then the serpent, sun

gleaming in his scales,
weaved through branches,
a ribbon of light. He spoke softly
in my ear, his hiss

insistent as an itch. The pulp
slipped between my breasts,
and it seemed the ground itself
fell away, recoiling

in a thick wisdom I never suspected.
In my dreams, I feel the kick
of promised pain within me,
and see her watching.

Her eyes gleam in shadow.
She smiles like she knew all along.

LILITH

Afterward, I journeyed through the desert.
No one saw me look back. My hair
curled behind me, dark as eons

before light, not her golden surrendering
tresses. Knowing I had no place
in the sun, I found shelter in the cool

depths of caves, where streams slip
from long-forgotten lakes, holding
secrets older than light. These caverns

I took for my inheritance. Some say
I was expelled, some that I flew from there
on demonic wings. I hold my tongue.

But one thing: escaping His curse,
I claimed the grit of life, all the mysteries
His foolish children call *myth*. Mine

are tales told in darkness, cries
of my children, those who drink deeply
from the cup of pleasure and pain

and savor the gift ordained for them:
this ecstasy they call damnation.

CAIN

I wake each morning haunted
by my dreams. Today, bruised sky
and threat of rain.

Blood poured from his head,
and I thought the earth would
never be sated.

It was over before
I realized it had begun.
What use are words?

I could tell you how I mourned,
how a life can fill with regret.
I feared for my life,

so He marked me, a curse
upon any who would
do me harm. I thought it a blessing.

Now, nothing remains but the slow
ache of the road, the dark eyes
of passersby who cross to the other side.

Yesterday, for the first time
in all this wandering, I knelt
to pray, and found nothing

but crushing silence. I think of my brother's
face, tell myself no judgment lasts
forever. Yet He has not spoken,

not since the Garden, and Abel
sits wordless beside me each night.

ABEL

Turning, I saw the rock, a dark sphere, arc
across the clouds. At once the sky was gone,
fields rose golden all around me, a red
stream cut jagged lines through the chest-high stalks.

Looking up, I found my brother standing
over me, his hands twisted, his eyes blank
as untilled earth. He dropped to my side,
clutching my cold hand. Our fingers entwined,

stained as one. What he had said, what I had said,
slipped away. His salt tumbled to the field,
where he knelt, a supplicant, his face
sun-cracked, etched in hungry shadows. At last

I saw him, my elder by minutes,
age suddenly, hunched, darkness coming on.

ANGEL AT THE GATE OF EDEN

These long years standing here,
shackled to this spot, Paradise
behind, the Sacred Rivers slipping
away from me, I stare across this valley
of unceasing change. They built
a tower stretching to heaven, a great
city which gleamed like Lucifer
in the pale light, until it was brought
low. Smoke rose for days. Each new
city fell quickly afterward.
Gabriel called mine a sacred
duty. *They must not be allowed to live
forever*, he said. Yet now I wonder
if I was ever needed, for this flaming
sword has never scorched flesh,
and they've yet to spare
a glance this way.

LUCIFER SPEAKS BEFORE GOD

His Sentence

What punishment is this?
      Take away my legs,
            and I will crawl

in the dust
      of their lives.
            This body,

though not glorified,
      will suit me well.
            I am content

to slither, to follow
      those You favored
            and expelled,

to watch them and see
      what all this might mean.

Discusses Job

Give a man all he asks, and he
      will praise you, no doubt.
            Give him a roof, scent

of baking bread,
      a lover in his bed,
            and he may be content.

They have forgotten
      what they lost,
            what they gained in the losing.

What do they know, do any
        of us know, of how deep
                we can sink, how often

our paths seem free
        until we look back.

                        Bruises His Heel

Looking at him, flayed,
        looking for You, thorns
                carving his skin, I wish

for tears red as his. I, first
        among creation, and still
                born too late to understand,

to take his place. Only he
        could bear Your wrath:
                my part was only

to set things moving.
        They will blame me for this,
                but I forced nothing.

You owe them enough
        to tell them they are free—
                as free, at least,

as the Morning Star.

Before the Final Battle

Will there be no resolution
        here for them? For us,
                their swords will ring

one final time. Their blood
        will pool like cattle's
                beneath the altar.

Behold them, guilty of nothing
        but choices. If they had any. Remember
                the Garden: two curious, naked

creatures, a changeless paradise,
        a tree which cries mystery
                over aching hills. Tonight

their stories end.
        Will You not at last
                speak? Will You not

tell us what You meant
        to plant here?

HIGHWAY 54:
AFTER DISCUSSING MY POETRY

The road builds rhythm,
steady hum of the engine,
enjambed thud

of expansion cracks
in pavement. Mile markers
make no judgments.

She told me *you write*
in tercets because
they're inherently unbalanced,

because they heighten your poem's
instability. Even your breaks—
so few end stops. Where

are you headed? Reading
you, I feel I'm scuttling
across a sand dune,

always falling, or fearing
the fall. Alone on the road,
half a thousand miles

from home, or a place
similar enough to pose,
I have no defense. The road

unfurls itself, the sky
presses its weight
upon me. Prairie

offers no consolation, winter
burrows through cracks
in the windshield. When

we fall from each other,
fall into silence
and other arms,

I will try to remember
our words, as though they
could ever save us. I will tell myself

they are enough. Soon,
I will retrace these miles,
a hawk will pose

voiceless questions, will turn
slow ellipses through the sky.

JOB FISHES WITH HIS FRIEND

All those who sin, suffer, Eliphaz says.
He does not say: therefore, you have sinned.

In the boat, the lake lulls
his friend's words to silence. In the days since god
took Job's children, his wealth, all he owned,
there has been no end to advice
from his wife, his friends. Now Eliphaz has asked
him to come fishing, said the air will soothe him.
Job waits in the prow of the boat, soot in his hair.
Ash like clawmarks streaks his face.
His friend casts the net across water.

Begged to repent, Job does not move. Overhead,
gulls cry, sharp, needful. Their shadows
on the water, its waves breaking on the boat, light
catching each crest, darkness and the cool pull
below: Job watches. His friend casts the net.
Fish drown in the bottom of the boat.

His friend speaks on. Job cannot hear him. The waves
wrap his thoughts, build rhythm. Later, when god
comes in wind and biting rain,
Job returns to whisper and shadows,
insistent tug of sea, bass slipping silent
outside the net's reach. When god speaks,
Job remembers the glistening net, heavy with fish,
rising from the sea's indifferent waves.

THE PESTILENCE

. . . e duro questo pistolenza fino a . . .
"in the midst of the pestilence there came to an end..."
    —Giovanni Villani

A third the world died, as the Revelation said.
A third the world died, black boils sprouting
from groins and armpits, Pestilence transmitted
by a glance, an evil eye. Grain wilted in fields,
bodies heaped outside doors, were dragged
to mass graves. Judgment was upon the land:
priests would not perform the rites.

Trapped by death in their monasteries
with no company but fleas and rats,
scribes despaired of anyone who would live to read
their accounts. The plague did not spare
the rich or the holy. Winter brought no respite.
Famine reigned.

Who could doubt the end of days? The world
was given over to Death. Devils slouched behind
desperate eyes. Parents fled from their children
and spared no thought for tomorrow. Nothing slowed
the sickness of the eastern wind.

Public mourning was banned, and all mourning
clothes. No one gathered together. Prayers
went unheeded. Villani's chronicle
stopped mid-sentence: *there came to an end...*

Yet pestilence ceased, and life resumed. Scholars
wrote little of the disease, turned their pens to War.
The Judgment passed: the condemned carried on.

IV.

HOW IT IS FOR EYELESS
THINGS IN CAVES

Maybe they wander in, foraging deep down
for food or seeking shelter, and they get lost far
beneath the surface. Or they decide
they like it in the dampness
of the earth, where predators venture
rarely, and sunlight does not scorch
them.
      Slowly they forget
the things they saw above, the harsh light
receding into memory,
into carefully forgotten dreams.
Then they lose sight itself
and creep along, cold as stone.
Their children are born
             knowing nothing else.

HENRY H. GODDARD
CONTEMPLATES HIS WORK
Ellis Island, 1913

Binet's scale proves my hypothesis:
the minds of men are regimented
as a rainbow's hues, fixed,
to be measured and evaluated,
laid out in rows, labeled:

idiot, imbecile, moron. Each has precise
meaning, a place in the world. But not
in the new world we must build,
for they recall lesser races,

ape-black men from Africa,
deficient Jews, Italians,
swarthy beings teeming Europe's east.
They swarm our shore, hungry,
desperate, deficient. A plague
infecting humanity, deadly
as influenza or cholera,

yet none had the courage
to speak its name. None, until I saw
the way, God's plain science
guiding my hand, his Word laid
in columns, ordered
by my hand in page
after page, a Gospel of human
order. Morton thought he saw it in skull
size, but I had the better number:

the measure of man's worth,
and proof—at last—
of our holy place
atop nature's highest peak.

MEDITATIONS ON THE PRESERVED

> *. . . and your*
> *tar-black face was beautiful.*
> —Seamus Heaney, "Punishment"

When I speak of them, I don't speak
of the pharaohs, who substitute planning
for fortune, but rather those
whom accident has blessed, ancient

ones secured in bogs, in glaciers,
or entombed in tar pits. Few
dodge by chance the slow teeth
of decay, yet among so many dead,

some remain, eternally beautiful, lingering
slow eons. They wait for us to unearth them,
for the camera and the appreciative eye,
for our sighs of admiration:

their bodies unmarred by age,
skin pulled taut over still-strong bones,
mouth upturned in what might be a smile,
as if they know something we've missed.

Though they died too young,
they never ask for pity, preferring only
to watch from empty sockets,
to watch us flicker past.

Highway 54: Controlled Burn

Eastern Kansas, hills pungent
with controlled burn: my eyes
sting, black clouds rise

into angry evening. All about me,
ribbons of flame unspooled
by grim-faced men with rusty

pickups. Sunglasses
conceal their eyes
as they watch the sky,

the night clear,
free of portentous clouds.
Rain will not come.

And if it did, they would still
burn, unwilling to risk
disaster, fires twisting

from these fallow
fields to those newly planted.
Sharp-lined faces know too well

mercy's cost, destroy
what they must to save
the rest. One man turns

his head to watch me pass,
glasses black as his hair
outlined against red flame,

orange sky. He nods,
I nod, accelerate
toward home, toward

whatever still remains.

WATCHING *CITIZEN KANE*

I'm reminded of my girl on the ferry
        (although I was nowhere near the water):
I was twelve, she was the mystifying
summer girl. I don't think I ever
found the nerve to speak to her,
though I did once choose her in red rover.

Now I think of the globe, spilling from Kane's hands,
Welles' camera explaining
that the whole world's trapped
within the memory of the lost, the unattainable

and I realize I've been there all these years
        (the objects have changed, not
        the fascination),
watching that globe like a seer's ball,
catching glimmers of things
                        outside my reach.

JESS WILLARD APOLOGIZES
TO JACK JOHNSON

These things I do not regret:
that I fought you, took your title.
That my right hand floored you in the 26th.
That you were 37, and I was young, strong.
That I was white.

I was just a Kansas cowboy,
just the white boy who finally knocked you down.

They offered me more money than I'd ever seen,
told me I was a savior,
Blue-eyed Jesus from the Great Plains.
I'd seen your swagger, heard your big talk.
You backed it up in the ring, though we choose
to forget. You bested white fighters,
married white women.
I hated you for all this.

So rich men in fancy suits turned us on each other
in one hundred degree heat,
made a fortune promoting, betting, scamming
as we battered each other until we could hardly stand.

These things I regret:
That we fought while you were on the run,
That they called me *Great White Hope*,
That when the crowd shouted *nigger*
I cheered them on.

You'd been long dead when a black man
with your fierce punches, your cocksure smile, stepped into the
        ring,
chanted your name. God, you would have been proud

to see those white folks panic. When Ali
called to you, I smelled upheaval
through the sweat and blood of the ring, a change buried
under the sweat and blood of what was coming,
what had come before.

I felt the ghost of your right hand when Watts burned,
felt each impact again with each napalm-drop
in Vietnam. It's always the same, Jack—rich folk
getting richer while we beat each other to hell.

When a heart attack dropped me, I held
my hand over my eyes the way you did, Jack,
that day I beat you. I thought the sky was on fire,
thought the world would end in the violence
I'd always known. They tell me I don't have long.

Ghost in the house, Ali yelled, and here you are.
I hated you because you took our title, our women. I hated you
and beat your face into a mass of blood. Forgive me, Jack.
I called you *nigger.*
I called them *sir.*

September 11th, 1973

I don't see why we need to stand by and watch a country go communist
because of the irresponsibility of its own people.
　　　—Attributed to Henry Kissinger

In '64, when Allende first ran,
we recognized the Chileans' choice
could threaten us all. An elected
socialist? We'd not stand
for it. We spent twenty million
keeping him out of office,
printed posters of children's
heads tattooed with hammer
and sickle, slick reminders
of the dangers of anti-Capitalist sentiment.

Allende won twice anyway. In '73,
when all our previous attempts at *coup*
d'état had failed, we brought the economy
crashing down, smuggled
tear gas and guns, parked
our ships off the coast,
sent spy planes overhead.

They stormed the presidential
home, and some say Allende pressed the hot
barrel of his rifle to his head.
That same day a stranded American on the streets
of Santiago met other Americans. Tanks
rolled down the streets. They told him
they were CIA, told him
we came to do a job, and it's done. Perhaps
they said too much.

A week later, five thousand were dead.
Pinochet held the country
in his sanctioned fist, sent
men to collect the American.
He vanished forever, like a flicker
on the edge of sight, gone
before we're sure it's there.

JOHN BROWN

. . . for I the Lord thy God am a jealous God, visiting the iniquity of
the fathers upon the children unto the third and fourth generation . . .
      —Exodus 20:5

A mural in the Kansas statehouse:
this man with wildfire eyes,
gun in one hand, Bible in the other,
his image iconic, recalling
a bloody sainthood:

The fires simmered
in Lawrence, the Free-State Press
heaped to ashes and charred
planks by the pro-slavers,
when he took four sons
and his burning abolition,
dragged five men from their homes,
and, in front of their families,
raised sharpened swords.

Brown spread his vengeance
like red wheat across fields,
left rubble of men behind him.
He stopped short of the prophet
who sent limbs to the four
corners of the land. Yet this man,
who carved wrath
across the state, was feared
by would-be southerners
all the way to the Colorado
border. The state broiled for years,
through skirmishes and lawlessness
and two nullified constitutions.

But Brown left,
raided Harper's Ferry,
and when we killed him
it was the proper Federal way,
on public gallows and rope
cutting against his neck.

MASADA

I

First, imagine a fortress which clings
to mountaintop, a road's jagged
cut carved from a thirteen-hundred
foot drop.
      See moonlight waver
on the Dead Sea's waves. Smell dust, blood,
soot from where the wind blew
the defenders' flame back upon them.
Notice the gleam of Roman shields
in the darkness before dawn. Look up
to highest hill of the crumbling fortress,
see Eleazar address his men. His beard shimmers
with sweat, his eyes burn in the night.
Do you see him, his sword cold
in his hands? Good,
              good. Now, listen to him speak:

II

They will come upon us tomorrow, and we
cannot stand against them. Our defenses have crumbled
since God turned our own fire against us,
destroyed our last hope. Shall we then be taken
and tortured, shall we watch our women raped,
our children enslaved? Shall we give ourselves
to the will of Rome, we who remember the holy city still,
though Roman fires smolder there, the House of God
left ruined and empty? See our punishment,
we who took innocent life along with guilty, who broke The Law:
now we see the vanity of our hopes. Yet life
is not the highest end of man. Let us spill our blood,
and that of our families (who we love with an abundance
of tears). Let us face the justice of the Almighty,
rather than our enemy's cruelty. See them below
us, their fires hungry in the night. We will give them nothing,
nothing but the ash and blood of our bodies.

III

See how they die: nine hundred and sixty.
They die like this: each man kisses his wife,
holds his children, then splits
their heads from their bodies.
Then ten men open the necks
of their fellow rebels, and one,
chosen by lot, bestows his mercy
on the other nine. This one, seeing
the deed done, sets ablaze
the possessions of the rebels
so the Romans will gain nothing,
and falls upon his own sword.
See each man lie with his family. See the blood
pool around them. See the black curl
of smoke, blacker even than the desert night. Hear
the crackle of fire on flesh. See skin melt away.

IV

Five escape the massacre—an old woman
and her children. Perhaps she tells
the Romans what took place, so they understand
what they see—a pyre, a baffling end to a war
the Jews had no chance of winning,
a mass grave and no clash of swords.
But she cannot tell the Romans what Eleazar said,
for women were not allowed near enough
to hear, and the deed was done in silence.

V

Now see Josephus writing this story. See him bent
over his parchment. See him give Eleazar the words
to convince his men, how he keeps their sword-arms
steady, how they hold their families' bodies, waiting
for the final blow. See how he imagines the last man studious,
checking for any who need the gift of another cut.
This man dies quickly, despite his unwieldy sword splitting him,
despite his entrails spilling out.

Imagined. No one who heard
what Eleazar said (or didn't say)
atop that doomed fortress
lived to report it. Yet here sits Josephus,
myth-making, one writer says, creating
a story for these dead. Centuries from now,
others will take this dead man's
stories and make them new. Some will call the rebels
terrorists. Some, *freedom fighters.*
His story will justify missile strikes on crowded
markets, bulldozers leveling
whole settlements. See armed guards on the wall.
See a car bomb littering
the dusty street with bodies, and how the missile
leaves a hissing wreck, a mother weeping.
See this on the nightly news.

VI

Now see me, writing this poem, telling you Josephus says *now I will tel*
not their story but the story of this people, who have seen their city ruined,
their temple burned, who have been scattered like ash. See this, though
he never wrote it.
                              And see me press my hands to the Wailing Wall,
last vestige of the Temple, though I have never been to Jerusalem.
See this faithless one kneel beside those who still believe.
See my feet smeared with ancient dust,
see me rise, see my pen cut across the page.
                                        Now stand with me ato
the cliff-face where some say rebels long ago killed
one another. Look with me across the moon-shunned night. The Dead
Sea, an obsidian blade, swallows light. Say a prayer, if you find peace
in such things.
                              I mourn the dead in my own, uncertain way.

PRESCRIPTION TO CURE
BINARY REASONING

Shine a flashlight on a globe. Note
the sharp divide of night and day. Trace
your finger across continents.
How easy, how perfect, is life distilled
to miniature. Reduction
holds that world together. Lines thin
as razor-wire form borders,
and tanks never ignore them,
never swallow blood and dust
beneath their treads.
Draw the line between us,
dear reader. How weightless to shoulder
the distance, to step into morning:
with all things diminished,
how simple our world would be.

Now walk the streets at sunset.
Trace the dusky divide
of our world, ambiguous borders
between countries, curve
of hip and thigh. Wake
in gray predawn sheets
and find your lover stirring,
worship the complexity
of lip-press and caress.
Let your hesitant bodies burn
in offering, worship of skin
which separates,
which holds us together.

I would like thank all those whose support and critical attention made these poems possible, including Thomas Fox Averill, Sarah Azizi, Michelle P. Baca, Marisa P. Clark, Nora E. Derrington, Dennis Etzel Jr., Amy Fleury, Melody S. Gee, Paul Gilbert, Jonathan Bohr Heinen, Chad Kurzawski, Sari Krosinsky, Juan J. Morales, Daniel Mueller, Mary Power, Karyn L. Smith, Kathryn Walkiewicz, Robert Wyckoff and Christina Socorro Yovovich;

my family, for their love and support;

the Woodley Press board, for making this book possible;

and particular thanks to Lisa D. Chávez, without whose wisdom and guidance this manuscript would not exist.

— *Israel Wasserstein*

About the Author

Israel Wasserstein was born and raised on the Great Plains and currently teaches at Washburn University in Topeka, KS. He received his MFA from the University of New Mexico in 2006.

About the Artist

The cover artwork, "Night Air" by **Jennifer Rivera**, was inspired by Wasserstein's poem "Foxwife" and appeared in the Art Afterwords collaboration between Rivera and poets from around Kansas. Rivera is an abstract expressionist painter from the Kansas City area who works primarily with acrylics on canvas. Known for edgy and emotionally evocative abstract paintings, she often employs the use of texture, bold strokes, and rich colors in her work. Her artwork has appeared in numerous magazines and was named one of Kansas City's Top Five Visual Artists in KC Magazine in 2010 and 2011. From Rivera's artist's statement: "To me, the marriage between the artist's freedom of expression and the viewer's freedom of interpretation is the fundamental beauty of abstract art and where inspiration can be found." Rivera's website is www.artistjenniferrivera.com.

www.ingramcontent.com/pod-product-compliance
Lightning Source LLC
Chambersburg PA
CBHW030156070426
42447CB00031B/728